Just
Enough
Difficult Topics
Made Easy

What Makes Us Unique?

Our First Talk About Diversity

Dr. Jillian Roberts

illustrated by
Cindy Revell

ORCA BOOK PUBLISHERS

Text copyright © Jillian Roberts 2016, 2021
Illustrations copyright © Cindy Revell 2016, 2021

Published in Canada and the United States in 2021 by Orca Book Publishers.
Originally published as a hardcover in 2016 (ISBN 9781459809482).
orcabook.com

Library and Archives Canada Cataloguing in Publication
Title: What makes us unique? : our first talk about diversity /
Dr. Jillian Roberts ; illustrated by Cindy Revell.
Names: Roberts, Jillian, 1971– author. | Revell, Cindy, illustrator.
Series: Roberts, Jillian, 1971- Just enough ; 3.
Description: Series statement: Just enough,
difficult topics made easy ; 3 | Previously published: 2016.
Identifiers: Canadiana 20200274759 | ISBN 9781459828254 (softcover)
Subjects: LCSH: Cultural pluralism—Juvenile literature. | LCSH: Difference (Psychology)—Juvenile literature. | LCSH: Toleration—Juvenile literature.
Classification: LCC HM1271 .R6 2021 | DDC j305.8—dc23

Library of Congress Control Number: 2020940402

Summary: A nonfiction picture book that introduces very young children to the concept of diversity in a way that is uplifting and approachable.

Orca Book Publishers is committed to reducing the consumption of nonrenewable resources in the making of our books. We make every effort to use materials that support a sustainable future.

Orca Book Publishers gratefully acknowledges the support for its publishing programs provided by the following agencies: the Government of Canada, the Canada Council for the Arts and the Province of British Columbia through the BC Arts Council and the Book Publishing Tax Credit.

Cover and interior artwork created digitally using Corel Painter.

Cover and interior artwork by Cindy Revell

Printed and bound in China.

24 23 22 21 • 1 2 3 4

This book was inspired by The Facts of Life app, a result of the creativity, skill and hard work of students and graduates at the Centre for Digital Media. Special thanks to Andrea Mayo, Tom Cheung, Sheva Shen and Paula Barcante. Thanks also to Brent Sternig and the Research Partnerships and Knowledge Mobilization unit at the University of Victoria—and the BCIC StartSmart voucher program—for providing significant support, guidance and resources to expand the reach and scope of The Facts of Life project. Without the collaboration of these amazingly inspired teams, the project would not have been possible.
Thank you!

The Facts of Life app is available for download.

For Kiersten.

—J.R.

For Tabitha, who thinks on a grand scale, and
Allan, the hardworking and hardplaying daredevil.

—C.R.

In nature, a rainbow is made beautiful by its different colors.

And just like that rainbow, the world is made beautiful because it's filled with many different kinds of people.

What makes us different?

People are different, or unique, in many ways. Some of these differences are things we can see on the outside.

People have different eye colors. They have different hair colors.
They have different skin colors.

People come in many different shapes and sizes too.
They can be tall or short. Big or small.

People also move, learn and communicate in different ways. Some people use a wheelchair to get around.

Some people need a guide dog to be their eyes or ears.
Some people talk to each other using sign language.

Other differences are harder to see, because they are on the inside. For instance, some people feel more comfortable alone or in small groups, while others like to be in big crowds.

We should always try to understand and respect people's different ways of being in the world.

What about different cultures?

Culture is a word we use to describe the shared attitudes, practices and beliefs of a certain group of people. Because there are many different cultures around the world, people speak different languages and practice different religions.

They also participate in different kinds
of traditions and celebrations.

What about differences at home?

People have different kinds of families. Some families have both a mom and a dad. Others have one mom or dad, or two moms or dads. Some children may be raised by a grandparent, stepparent or other loving caretaker. Some families live together, and others live in separate homes.

Are there other kinds of differences?

Yes—many! People have different kinds of jobs. People live in different kinds of homes and wear different kinds of clothes. People eat different kinds of food and take part in different activities or hobbies. There are also different ways people show love and take care of each other.

What do these differences mean?

Because each of us is unique, we may not always agree with or understand someone else's beliefs or choices. We may not like to dress the same way, eat the same food or take part in the same kinds of activities.

Even though there are things that make each of us different, we are all equally important. We all deserve love, respect and compassion, regardless of what we look like or how we live our lives.

The truth is, we are much more alike than we are different.

We all want to learn.
We all want to laugh and grow and explore.

We all want to spend time with our families, be loved and make friends.

We all want to be treated nicely by the people around us.

The world becomes a much more beautiful place
when we celebrate what we have in common.

And what makes us unique!

Just A Few More Questions

Why do some differences make us feel scared or nervous?

Sometimes differences make us uneasy because they are new to us, or we don't understand them properly. Talking about our differences is a good way to make them less scary. And thinking about all the things that make us the same can help too! The next time you meet someone who seems really different from you, try thinking about all the things you have in common as well as what's unique.

What about people of different sexual orientations?

Sexual orientation refers to who we are attracted to. Girls can be attracted to boys or girls, and boys can be attracted to boys or girls. It's important to treat people with respect and kindness regardless of their gender or who they are attracted to. We all have the right to be ourselves and love whomever we want.

What are racism and prejudice?

Racism is the belief that people of certain races are somehow better or worse than others. A racist person might act in a hateful way or treat someone differently because of the color of their skin.

Prejudice, sometimes called *stereotyping*, is having a negative attitude toward or belief about someone based on their race or other traits—like gender, religion, age, class, body type, sexual orientation or ability.

It is never okay to act in a way that is racist or prejudiced, which is also known as *discrimination*. If you see someone being treated unfairly or bullied because they are different, you should speak up or tell an adult you trust.